Rene

MW01015955

Keep up the good work
Brother!

Norm

KEEPING 6

NORMAN SHARKEY

BALBOA.
PRESS
A DIVISION OF HAY HOUSE

Balboa Press books may be ordered through booksellers or by contacting:

Balboa Press
A Division of Hay House
1663 Liberty Drive
Bloomington, IN 47403
www.balboapress.com
1-(877) 407-4847

ISBN: 978-1-4525-6306-0 (e)
ISBN: 978-1-4525-6305-3 (sc)
ISBN: 978-1-4525-6307-7 (hc)

Library of Congress Control Number: 2012921509

Printed in the United States of America

Balboa Press rev. date: 11/19/2012

KEEPING 6

Shirley

"6 UP" is an expression used on the streets to alert someone that the authorities are approaching. The person sounding the alert is considered to be "Keeping 6". The "6 Recovery Values" are the warning method we use to avoid being caught up in active drug use again. To the degree that we "Keep 6" every day will determine just how ""Happy Clean"" our life will continue to be. As you well know, there are many other resources available to you while dealing with recovery but, whatever method you use, you will discover that it must be applied every day in order to get the best results. We wanted the best high available when we were using so why wouldn't we want the best high available in our clean life? If we are simply drug free but not very happy, eventually we will find ourselves going back to using. If we seriously apply whatever recovery methods we have been introduced to, every day, we will begin to discover real happiness for ourselves as well as our families and real friends.

Joey

CHAPTER 1

We admitted we were powerless over any kind of drugs and our lives had become a MESS!

It appears that addicts themselves are the only ones who can't see that Recovery Value 1 describes their past, present and future destinations! Even after many years of out of control drug use, which is evident to anyone and everyone who is not a user (especially those who love you) we will insist we are ok. What does ok, mean to an addict? It usually means I have enough dope for today or, I can pan-handle, steal, or use someone so I will have enough dope for today! As long as I am stoned or can get stoned I am ok. But you're going to lose your family! No I won't, I am ok! You're going to lose your job! No I won't, I'm ok. You just got fired! Who cares, I am ok. You're going to jail for robbing that pizza driver. Who cares, I am ok. You're one day out of jail. You get stoned and beat your wife, terrorize your kids, and trash your house! You're going back to jail! Who cares, I'm ok. After 2 days out of the joint, you hold up a corner store. Back to the slammer! Who cares, I am Ok. You're out again, NOT FREE, because you're still using, just out on the street. No one wants to see you except others who are as messed up as you are! Who cares, I am ok. I don't need people. Any spare change? Thanks you Goof! Some jerk stole my blankets last night. I'll get more today from the shelter. As long as I can see someone more screwed up than me, I am ok. As long as there are suckers to use, I am ok. Where does it usually end? Death, prison or insanity, that's where. We live in delusions from our past. We seem to think there is plenty of time to change, if we have to! Can we believe that? We say; "if we have to". Like, what's the problem? I have often said that nothing can degrade us the way drugs can and still have us believe they are our best friend. Is there a person alive who can get us to do the things the way drugs can get us to do and then go back for more?

This first example is the person who ends up accepting life living on the street, as though it is a very normal existence. The street will eventually kill that person.

The second example of an addicted person is the one who has managed to keep it together enough and has not lost much materially. They are employed, earn better than average money, have many of the material things that go with steady employment, are able to show up for work most of the time and do an acceptable job. They socialize with other employees who are also regular users and, as a result, tell themselves that their drug use is not a problem. When they are passed over for a promotion, they say they don't want it anyways, (not much), or the person who was promoted was sucking up to the boss! They refuse to see that their production on the job has decreased, or that their superiors are aware that they're just going through the motions day to day. They have a few drinks at lunch or a few tokes during the afternoon or morning breaks and head for the neighborhood bar after work. Not every day, because they are still trying to keep it together, but more and more often, as time goes by. These people may even hang onto their jobs until they retire at which point the addiction will completely take over. No bosses, no deadlines, no calling-in sick. Freedom! Would you call this person a success?

Next, we have the pre-teen and the teenager who are completely different from the first two. Drug addicted is a phrase that they can never accept because they don't fit that image. The expression most commonly used is "party!" If they progress into addiction it will be "party time" all the time. In my own case, as a 14 year old starting high school, I was overwhelmed by the size of the school; the cool, confident, older teenagers who looked like they had it all together. They didn't. They just looked that way to me. Many of them were well into their drug careers. They were not cool. Drugs gave them that image. Without drugs they were as insecure as I was. I had no way of knowing that at the time. I thought what

I saw was real. I wasn't the first and I won't be the last kid to fall for the image and the glitter.

People like me will agree, (with very few exceptions), that life after their first high was never the same. From then on, everything in my life involved chasing that high. That became the most important thing in my life. Without realizing it, I let nothing stand between me and my objective of being high. Anything else in life was unimportant. Sports, which were my life up to then, suddenly became kid games. Family was no longer family; just strangers to live with. School was only important because that's where my drugs and using friends were. Drugs and sex were my life. I floated along like this for about four years, and then got kicked out of school. That's when the drug use really took off. No one could make me see where I was heading. The minute they brought up my using, I turned them off. From then on, I progressed to the other two examples of an addict. Sometimes working and appearing to have it together, other times, living on the street.

After years of being drug free I can now understand the helplessness my family and friends felt watching me slowly destroying myself and anyone who cared for me. I was so lost I could not see or feel their pain. Anyone who spoke against drugs immediately became my enemy. People lied for me, made excuses for me, gave me money, a place to stay, food, and every possible convenience they could afford but, they could have given me their souls and it would never have been enough. What a trail of misery I left behind. I did not intend to have people hurt; they just were because they cared. That was their only shortcoming; they were in the way.

If you have someone in your life like me, I wish I could offer some quick magic solution but, I have to say, the addict will not stop his or her insane journey until there is no one left to use. I know this does not sound very encouraging to anyone who is trying to help but simply let him or her know that when they've had enough, your door is open to them. You will probably go crazy with guilt, which is what addicts create in people who care about them, but you must stand your ground or be bashed about some more. As humans, we can only do so much. As they say; you can lead a horse to water, but you can't make her or him drink. However, don't take the water away because they may get thirsty later.

Someone, somewhere, in our world today, is being introduced to drugs for the first time. Their life is about to take on a drastic change, and not for the best either, the odds of them or their families being able to live a normal life again are slim, if any. If they are the type of people who need some additive in their body in order to feel good, they're in trouble.

Roger-Bob

CHAPTER 2

Through being open and honest with fellow addicts we come to know a power we can depend on called God!

If we completely believe that, in order to live a successful life, we must be free from the drugs we used to avoid reality, we must then adopt a plan to stay free from drugs. Perhaps you think you can avoid reality and still be successful. Maybe you can on a material level but, if you are avoiding reality, you are avoiding life. You will be on a different wavelength than 90 percent of the world. This causes problems in communication.

Let us assume that you want to be part of the answers to life's problems instead of the creator of confusion. Values two though six will give you the framework to live a happy, contented, drug free life. No one I know has been able to follow these values to perfection from day one to the end of their life! Life can get very confusing at times and no one can cause confusion like an addict in recovery. Small things can be turned into gigantic problems. These six values are guidelines to hang onto when the tornadoes in life hit us.

"Open and honest", when I was using, was for losers. If you want to get thrown out of school, fired, divorced or go to jail, then be open and honest. The way to avoid all of the above was to lie my way out of it. No one admitted the truth, are you out of your mind? I wasn't even honest with myself, so why should I be honest with you? That was part of being solid. Solid, you know? What I'm trying to say here is that my way of stumbling though life was not bringing the results I wanted. I wasn't sure what I wanted, but I knew I wanted a lot more happiness than I was getting. Why do I have to be open and honest with other addicts? What's in it for me? If I'm open and honest with people, they won't think I'm the big man I am pretending to be. That was my life. Pretending. Things I wanted people to see were only an image. Without the image, what was I? That was scary. At that point, I had to decide if I wanted to continue my clean life or go back where I came from.

Regardless of how long I'm clean, this is a continuous decision I must consider when I do something dishonest or sneaky. I'm talking about me now, so don't think I'm starting to preach. Each of us will discover how open and honest we will have to be in order to feel contentment in our guts. Some of the things that bother me may not bother you and vice versa. This is where I have to be honest with me and you have to be honest with you. My head can tell me that what I'm doing is ok but my guts may tell me the opposite. One of the most important things I've learned over the years, through trial and error, is to listen to your guts and not your head. My head is what I want to do; my guts are what God wants me to do. If I decide to do something and my guts start to rumble, if I'm wise, I will talk to someone before I go against the warning I'm getting from inside. However, as that old saying goes, some people learn from other people's mistakes. However, most people have to be the other person.

Why are we so pig headed (nothing against pigs) and determined to prove anyone and everyone wrong? Why is it we will listen to bad advice very willingly and reject advice that will allow us to discover true happiness for the first time in many years, perhaps ever? In my case, I rejected most good advice because it looked too difficult to follow or meant that I would have to change my living habits, which I was not ready to do. Sometimes I rejected good advice because I didn't respect the people who were offering it. Over the years, as a result of some attitude rehab, I have been able to simply evaluate the advice and leave the people's personalities out of it. Good advice is good advice regardless of who is delivering it. When I was using, I would have taken advice from Hitler and been positive it was good. My decision to live drug free meant I would have to do a lot of changing in my thinking and living habits.

Open and honest, I knew, would be an absolute requirement, as opposed to closed and sneaky. I finally realized I was the one I was running from. As a result of getting a little more open and honest, I became a little more relaxed and contented. Even a pea brain like mine began to understand that if I wanted more contentment I would have to be more open and honest. People who have tried this way of living are probably smiling as they read these words because it is only when you have tried being open and honest that you will understand why, those of us who have been such sneaks, cannot stay comfortably clean otherwise. In the end, each of us has to decide how open and honest we will be. This is one walk I, and you, have to walk on our own. I don't live inside you and you don't live inside me, therefore, each of us is responsible for our own contentment. I'm greedy and I want a lot of contentment so I need to practice a lot of honesty. Honesty equals clean conscience equals a contented head and guts.

In my life, today and for many years now, I only have to check my honesty level. Sometimes, if I'm overly tired, I may have the beginning of a headache but all I have to do is close my eyes for a few minutes and it goes away. For a cold or flu, that method doesn't work but it does for a headache, provided my conscience is clear.

You may wonder what things you need to be honest about. If you smell because you haven't showered for a week, do you have to ask someone why you smell? We are the same people who didn't want anyone telling us how to live, (remember)? So then, why are we suddenly ready to have someone live our lives for us now? I am the one who wants a contented life so I have to decide on my level of honesty. If someone told me to be honest about something and I was and it blew up in my face I would blame them and be convinced that honesty was a lot of crap. There may be some things in your past, concerning good friends or relatives, that you may want to talk to them about. If you do:

1. Make sure you are determined to stay clean.

2. Be ready for any unexpected reactions from them and don't try to justify what it was you did.

If you are sincere about staying clean, I know the results will amaze you. People are more forgiving of us guys than perhaps they should be. It was at times like that when I made my first discoveries of God being there with me. He's not pushy. He will only be part of my life if I want him to be. People are the ones who are pushy, not God. I will repeat the following a few times throughout this book. If, at any time, you get screwed up as a result of a suggestion you have read and tried to follow from this book, find someone who has been clean awhile and talk to them. Perhaps the advice is not for you at this time or at anytime. Different strokes for different folks. Because you get confused over something doesn't mean you have to get stoned. Talk to someone. Deal? The only purposes for this book is to help you stay clean, so don't rush into something unless you understand the directions. I am assuming you are attending or have attended a meeting at Narcotics Anonymous or Cocaine Anonymous. You must have talked to people from these groups whom you can identify with, so bounce some things off them. They can definitely ease your confusion. Open and honest, one day at a time, will slowly begin to connect you with the Great Spirit, Higher Power, Jesus, and Buddha, Mohammad or God as you begin to understand them. If you have had any previous religious experiences that have been positive, you may want to reunite with them. I will try to describe to you the ups and downs (mostly ups) of my discovering God as I now understand God. I am one of many people who thought that God was a sick joke, laid on me by my parents, to scare me into being good.

At one time, when I was in the army, I stood up on a table stoned and said "if there is a God, let Him strike me dead now." I read somewhere that some other fool had done that one time and so thought it would make me look like a hero. Even as I said those words I was not so sure He wouldn't strike me dead. Everyone in that bar thought I was something else. I was. I was an idiot. I have since come to understand that God has more important things to do. Taking the life of a drug addict who was killing himself was not one of them. He's still up there laughing.

On the 6th of June 1971, I came-to, in a flop-house room with pains in my chest and thought it was a heart attack. I fell out of bed, onto my knees, and asked God to save my life. My last bargain with him was "if you do, I'll get clean." He delivered and, so far, so have I. One day at a time, I have not had the craving or the need to get stoned since that day. I believe God saw that I was serious and also knew I was scared I was going to die. So, he stepped up to the plate and hit a home run for me. I wish I could say I have lived a perfect life since then, but I can't. I am not well, but am I ever better. I understand today that progress, in all areas of my life, is what is important. Perfection comes after this life.

God and Alcoholics Anonymous saved my life and gave me the tools I needed to stay drug free. I was happier than I have ever been in my life, but I wasn't very real. That's when I was introduced to a drug program outside of Montreal called Spera. The founder and director of the program was a man who gave me the opportunity to get real and discover who I was. I will be eternally grateful to Jerry and Sharon Burton for the eye-opener they gave me. Also, Charlie McGarrity and Eddie Maloney, who were great guys. I love you. Everyone I met there played a apart in me discovering who I was. Continuing to discover daylight, one day at a time, is where it's at for me today.

As the clean days added up, so did my understanding of God. In 1975, I was at an A.A meeting with a good friend of mine, Bill Main. Another member had been telling me about a Christian community that he would like me to visit and I kept making-up excuses as to why I couldn't. Again, that day, he said "Norm, why don't you come see these people?" Before I could say anything, Bigmouth Bill said "can I go too?" I was very nervous about "Jesus freaks", (not that I knew any), so I didn't know what to expect. We got to the house about four in the afternoon and I thought we'd be gone by four thirty. We finally left at midnight. People talked about Jesus as though he was sitting right there with us. Their eyes sparkled and I was positive they were stoned. I must say, it was electric. I left there with my head spinning but the rest of me felt like I had been given another clue in my ongoing search for connecting. Bill is now, and has been for many years, the director of a very successful drug rehab program in Ottawa called Harvest House.

Like a kid in a candy store, I went to every Christian church I could find. Sometimes I got confused or hurt by some Christian people and swore I would never go back. Jesus is patient and I finally understood the one important message that Jesus came to deliver; love God, love your neighbor and love yourself. If I'm doing that, I'm doing it all. There are many days when I've missed the mark on all of those but I get up and take a run at them again the next day. Love is the greatest! If your understanding of God does not include love for your brothers and sisters, perhaps you need to ask yourself why? God loves us and wants us to love him but we can only do that if we love people.

I mention my experience with Jesus because he was the human example of love in action on this earth. I am not trying to convert anyone to Jesus. He is the God of my understanding. That doesn't mean I'm right or wrong. To put it simply, that is how I relate to God. I must also add that when I'm loving people, I really feel his presence and I am not alone. Never! I have dragged Him through some awful places since 1975, but He never left me. That is love folks. This world of ours seems to be more concerned with who is right or wrong instead of "how much do we love?" Am I describing anyone you know?

This discovery of god, for each of us, is a never-ending journey that we all will surely walk. If we are to discover love we must discover our God. Again, this is simply my experience. You will also have a story, which may include Buddha, Mohammad, The Great Spirit or others, whom you think are just as necessary as Jesus in your life. To that I say, as I say to myself; "just don't forget the love."

I believe the most important thing we all need to leave as our legacy is love for our brothers and sisters, world-wide. Open and honest leads us to God, and God leads us to our brothers and sisters. I had to become an addict to learn this. I hurt an awful lot of people in the process. One day at a time, I've been trying to balance the scales. Remember, one more time; open, honest and love. If you're not sure how to start connecting with this mysterious power, simply go off, by yourself, and start talking as you would to a good friend. He knows when you are serious so, do not waste anymore time thinking about it, just do it. Strangers are his specialty.

Jen

CHAPTER 3

With the help of God and our friends, we took an honest look at ourselves and became willing to change the things that were keeping us high.

In recovery value two, we get an idea of whom and what God is and how to begin our relationship with him. Recovery Value 3 says; "with the help of God and our friends." Who exactly are our friends? Do we have any? Have we ever had any? Do we really know the difference between friends and enemies? You do? I didn't. Most of the people whom I thought were my enemies, when I was using, were actually my friends and, most of the people whom I thought were my friends became my enemies when I stopped using. Our motto, when we were using, was; watch that clean guy, he will stab you in the back every time. I really used to believe that. Just goes to show how whacked I was. To me, a friend was anyone who thought drugs were good. Aren't you glad I wasn't choosing your friends? You chose yours the same way? If that is true, perhaps we should take a better look at what a friend really is.

When I was a little boy, there were many kids I played with and they were called my friends. I know there were times when I went home with a bloody nose and times when my friends went home with a bloody nose. Within a few days, we were best of friends again. Forgiving and forgetting came pretty easy at that age. As I grew a bit older, grudges were tougher to give up. Image and pride were becoming important in my life. I did not know how to be a good loser or a good winner. If I lost, I had plenty of excuses. If I won, I would take great pleasure in humiliating the loser. Would you say I was immature, with an attitude like that?

During elementary school, sports, and trying to improve in sports, were my reason for living. Making a good play, intercepting a pass for a touchdown, catching what looked like a home run ball, continually boosted my ego. The friends I had, on any given team, were real friends as far as I was concerned. I still believe that many years later. Sports are much like the military; they teach you discipline, competitiveness and comradeship; one for all and all for one.

As I mentioned in Recovery Value two, when I arrived at high school, the school was bigger. There were more students, bigger guys, and better athletes. It was much like grade one in elementary school. Time to prove you fit in all over again. That, as I understand things today, is the way life is meant to be. Continually proving you belong. I did ok, I felt accepted. I was accepted. I had friends and believe to this day that they really were friends. I haven't seen any of my high school friends in years but that is my fault, not theirs. They were good buddies.

In today's life, what is my idea of a friend? This is what I call a friend; a person who knows everything about me, good and not so good, and loves me anyway. In order to take an honest look at myself in Recovery Value three, I needed people who would help me see through the fog and the lies. I needed to be prepared to accept the truth about myself. As most addicts do, I tried to give people the impression I was ok and that I just did a little too much dope. There are many things that caused me to use and kept me high. From July 1967 until the 6th of June 1971, I was in and out of recovery 5 times. I went to meetings until they were coming out of my ears but I didn't do any changing. I didn't use, that was about it. I smiled, said all the right things at the meetings, and somehow thought it would rub off on me. I didn't realize I had to rub it into myself. Even with a load of baggage, drugs can help you stay a bit mellow. Without drugs, I just had the raw nerves sticking out in everyone's way. Unless the baggage came out, I could not know clean and happy. My secrets kept me sick and lost.

Through the Spera Program, I was able to see that my secrets weren't any different from anyone else's. Spera allowed me to get real. Other programs helped me to get drug free, but Spera showed me what real was. I completely believe that my God, as I understand Jesus today, was responsible for directing me to Spera. The right place, at the right time. What were the things that kept me high? I thought that I was out of control and my life was a mess because I used drugs. This was a fact but I also used drugs because my life was a mess. The more it seemed that drugs could ease the pain and make me feel like I was great, grand and wonderful, the more drugs I used. I don't know at what point in my teenage years I felt I didn't measure up with other guys. All I know is that, when I was stoned, I felt equal or maybe even better. The angel of my dreams; when stoned and, the devil of my fears; when not stoned. These were the two things that continually stopped me from honestly looking at myself. My ego, (the angel of my dreams), said; "you're ok, just don't use dope." My Fear said; "If you do look, you won't' be able to handle it, just leave it alone, it will go away by itself."

For years, drugs allowed me to avoid myself. Clean, I couldn't. When I couldn't handle the pressure any longer, I would go back to drugs. I don't know if that is the same for everyone who goes back to using, but that was my pattern. When I finally realized I didn't have the legs to run anymore, I decided to get serious.

Let's look at the seven deadly sins. For me, they were deadly and would definitely lead to lots of flowers or insanity; 1- pride, 2- greed, 3- lust, 4- anger, 5- gluttony, 6- envy and

7- laziness. These were not things I was too anxious to admit to or look at. Who is?

1. **Pride**, if it is healthy, is something we must have if we are to survive. Most of my pride was not the healthy kind. In my mind, I was proud of using people, where, in fact, I was the one getting used. In order to use people, I had to use drugs to kill my conscience. I knew nothing about "keep your conscience clear and have no fear." Drugs removed fear like freezing your tooth removes pain. I thought I could use the freezing to avoid digging out the decay. I had to look at the ego and turn it into healthy reality. I could only do that if I continued with the next seven.

2. **Greed**. Another unhealthy thing that goes with greed is selfishness. I tried to show people I was very unselfish only to, time after time, show them the opposite. Unselfish addict is an oxymoron, or should I say, if you believe an addict is unselfish, you are a moron. We are the people who are screaming that we can't stand this selfish world while each day we contribute to the selfishness. If I shared anything with anyone, it was because I wanted to look like a big man, or I was setting them up for something.

3. **Lust** goes hand in hand with Greed. What a useless, frustrating game this is. All the fantasies that go on in our minds while this game is being played out! Our blood pressure probably triples and our pulse almost jumps out of our body. We become sleep-walking zombies. Hypnotized!

Sex; the only thing, other than drugs, that can reduce us to mush. Not you? Ok, me. Sex is very much a part of our life. I discovered sex with love and, when I did, guilt connected to sex was gone. Love has everything to do with it. We have to respect people or feel guilty.

Once, during my using days, as a result of wanting and needing drugs, I performed oral sex on a man. This caused the type of guilt that only more and more drugs could dull, to some degree. This also caused me to question my sexuality and my ability to have any kind of real relationship with a female. As long as drugs were in the picture, I could never find the answer.

4. **Anger**. Are you kidding? Me? Angry? Nothing bothered me, except every stupid clean person. With their big houses, cars and bank accounts. Guys; better looking and better built and the girls who hung around with them. All the phony church people and their clean, polished kids. Is there anything to compare with Sunday morning coming down? The suits, walking around with their arrogant bare faces hanging out. Anger is too mild a word. For me it was hate. The injustice of it all! I had it all; the power of negative thinking. What a power it is too. I talked negatively. This only led to more anger and hate. When I got clean, I slowly began to see that the anger and hate that I felt were at myself for the way I was wasting my life.

5. **Gluttony**. Don't be such a pig! Poor old pig gets it again. Doing things to excess; sex, drugs, food, cigarettes, cars,

house, clothes, laughter, and sadness. Too much was just right. I still do some things to excess and probably will till the day I die. Come on now. Life is simple! If I don't try to grab everything my head tells me I need, I can go to bed and have a peaceful contented sleep. Then, get up tomorrow and grab everything – not! This is a lifetime work-out we are on folks! One day at a time. Cut yourself a little slack, but not for too long!

6. **Envy**. I wasn't envious of anyone! Not much. In my mind, anyone who had something I didn't, (which was almost anything), probably ripped it off or killed them for it. If it was a girl, it was because he had more drugs. God, I was sick and hateful. I couldn't accept that some people got things legally and because they worked hard. In reality, sometimes people do get things they don't deserve but they usually find ways to lose them too. I'm sure I don't deserve everything I've got, but I'm sure glad I didn't get what I deserved. Today, I honestly mean this, if someone is living a decent life, I don't envy them. I try to copy them. I get rewards when I do.

7. **Laziness**. Drugs made me lazy. My mind was continually scheming but my body was lazy. Nothing was important except sex, drugs and rock and roll, and not too much rock and roll. I worked when I ran out of excuses, but I usually found a way to get laid off so that I could draw U.I.C, or whatever it's called today (unemployment insurance benefits). I had no ambition, no confidence and no desire to get any work. That is where drugs deposit you; a lump with a joint

in one hand and a syringe or beer in the other. We are blood suckers who resent the world because they allow us to be where we are. Get a haircut and get a real job – right! I believe every human being is bothered, to some degree, by the seven deadly sins but, for addicts, it is an out of control epidemic. We probably will never eliminate these things from our life but we must find ways to control them. Every day, one or more of these attributes raise their ugly head trying to devour me but God, as I understand Him, continues to pull me through the day clean. I have made a lot of mistakes since I've been clean and probably hurt and disappointed some people but, as long as I stay clean, I have, hopefully, the chance to repair any damage. Stoned only creates more damage and kills me at the same time.

Relapse: I had many excuses as to why I returned to using. Today, I can see that I wasn't prepared to change certain things about my lifestyle. I was clean but still a very lost person as a result of my years of using. From the age of 14, drugs were my teacher, until I made my first attempt at recovery when I was 30. This amounted to 16 years of living in the illusion that convinced me no one was honest or real except people who used. As I mentioned earlier in this book, I had to almost die before taking this recovery stuff seriously. Prior to my last relapse in 1971, I had been clean for about 6 months; not very happy, but clean. Then, my marriage broke up and I found myself looking for companionship and comfort but mostly "sex". I knew bars offered a lonely person companionship so that's where I went. I had no experience at picking-up women clean so I decided to drink alcohol. What I was looking for happened and, for a few days, I thought I had made the right decision and life was good. I had about four days off from work and when I was due to go back to work I decided to use my sick days in order to extend my well deserved party. After four or five days of calling-in sick, I decided to get clean again but I discovered that the guilt and fear brought on by the knowledge I had received from other recovery programs kept me using. Then came the morning when, at the age of 34, I thought I was having a heart attack. The message was finally received.

I am not the only addict who has thrown away their recovery because of sex. Over the years, working with other addicts, I have seen it happen over and over again. I understand that people can get discouraged and disappointed with their lives and go back to using but they will then usually try recovery again and deal with the problems or change what needs changing.

Recovering addicts get into relationships with other recovering addicts before either of them has looked inside themselves and, in most cases, disaster occurs. One or both, being dissatisfied with the other and not realizing it is themselves they are dissatisfied with and then go back to using. Neither wants to admit that sex is the big attraction in the relationship. Sex is good but a relationship will fall apart if that is the main building block. Until we look at and change the flaws in our personality and discover who we really are we are going to be attracted to the physical needs that another can fulfill for us and we can give them and, in time, we will get tired of that person as we would an old toy and then move onto another, more exciting challenge. We are kids in a candy store when it comes to sex.

In bars, on the street, in high society, even in prisons, drugs open door to sex. By the way, alcohol is probably the most common drug and, it's legal. Heroin, cocaine, crystal meth, crack (which is really cheap), ecstasy and other drugs are specifically developed to help us sexually. I am not telling any former or presently using addict anything they don't already know with this information. This is more intended for the person who may be having a hard time understanding why someone is prepared to waste their life and destroy their family when all they have to do is get into recovery somewhere.

When we do enter recovery we act like little kids if someone brings up the topic of sex. We either giggle or make some smart ass comment such as "the only sex problem I have is that I am not getting any", or, we get angry and say sex has nothing to do with our drug use. I am not an expert on sex but I do know that it took up a lot of my thinking and energy without me being completely aware of the fact that I was allowing it to run my day. The game playing we do in our minds, just walking down the street, can quite easily have us walk into a bar and relapse within minutes.

I know many people will say I am obsessed with sex but you explain to me why people will throw their lives away when opportunity for success is available to them. Drugs will eliminate the conscience as well as the person!

Sam

CHAPTER 4

Since we had harmed many people,
we attempted to make things right with them.

Since we had harmed, harmed, harmed! How about tore the
guts or heart or life out of many people. Is that not a little
more like it? We have no idea. Will we ever really know just
how much we hurt people? Because they love us so much, they
will try to protect us from the truth. Most people will say "I'm
just happy to see you clean," giving us the impression that
no damage was done. Since we weren't really super anxious
to sit down, for a few hours or a day, and have our insanity
laid out in front of us, we gladly take "I'm glad you're clean"
and go happily on our way. I read somewhere that addicts are
very sensitive people. Perhaps towards ourselves we are but,
when it comes to other people, we are usually very sensitive
after we have been busted for something or our gold fish

dies. When it comes to someone else's guts, it is hard to see the sensitivity in action. We can't possibly understand what we have inflicted on other people because we have had our feelings and nerves insulated with the dope we were doing. They just had the raw nerves that we were pounding on. We were grade-A butchers, cutting the life, slice by slice, out of the people who gave us life. Yeah, our parents are usually the first ones to feel our hate. We don't see them as the people who have given us life. We, for whatever reasons, see them as the ones responsible for our pain. Everyone's parents have, in some way, not met the needs of their children, but there is a good chance they could say the same about their parents. We aren't, our parents aren't, and their parents aren't, God. We seem to think everyone else should be like God, but it's ok if we are just human. We in fact accept that it's ok to be less than human. Sitting down with our parents is especially important for them so they can release the guilt they have also been carrying. Whether real or imagined, they must have the opportunity to clean their side of the table. "Where did we go wrong" has to be answered so both you and your parents can start to love each other, perhaps for the first time!

In my case, my poor mother had to endure a husband and two sons who were addicts. She somehow lived into her seventies, but happiness was not something she experienced on a regular basis. My father was a clergyman and a very good one at that. He was also an alcoholic, a very good one too. I remember my mother saying, once they were divorced,

"I could have accepted his drinking if he had been working at any other job but, preaching about God on Sunday and living the devil's life the rest of the week was eventually too much for me." Even then, she stayed with him until all three of her kids were out on their own. I was in the military and received some medals for my service but my mother was the person in our family who deserved medals. I know I will never be aware of the crap she had to go through just to try and give us some semblance of a sane childhood. I was not aware, until about the age of 14, just what she sacrificed to try and protect us from the embarrassment and shame of an alcoholic preacher father. Then, she watched helplessly as my brother and I went down the same road. I even had the arrogance to try to make her feel guilty for getting a divorce, telling her, when I was stoned, that I needed them to be together so I could feel I still had a family. I, I, I, I, I, I, I needed but not what was best for my mother. If my mother wasn't crazy, it wasn't because my brother, my father, and I didn't do everything possible to make her that way.

My father, since he was telling people about God, in my mind, had to be nothing less than perfect. Every day, people told me how much they respected him and how great he was and I expected him to live up to that image. Even if he hadn't been an addict he, nor anyone else, can completely live the image we expect of them. My motto was; easy on myself, critical of everyone else. I could do whatever I wanted in life but everyone else had to follow the 10 commandments. As my addiction progressed, one thing that rattled my cage was when someone would say; "you're just like your father." They didn't mean father God either. As my habit grew, I was completely convinced it was all because of my dad. Once again; easy on me, critical of others. That was the only way I could justify my growing addiction. I'm ok, they're not ok. "What do they expect?" "Look at the example I was given!" These are excuses addicts from addicted families use. On the other hand, addicts from families where no drugs of any kind were used will say: "My parents were too strict. Not even a little bit of alcohol was allowed. That's why I rebelled and started to use!" There are millions of excuses in the "naked city" and we addicts have invented most of them.

At the same time that we must take responsibility for our addiction and we are getting deeper and deeper into it, confusion in the home and family certainly creates good breeding grounds for drugs. The breakdown of any family has to be shared by all. Even though I was convinced I was ok, my attitude, like the attitude of any beginning addict, played out with rebelling, anger and temper outbursts, running away from home etc, etc. I could see my family coming apart, me coming apart, and it climaxed when I was expelled from high school. Most of us want to see our family function but I was not ready to change my lifestyle or do anything to stabilize things. Like I would do from then on, I ran away from the situation and joined the military. My brother and sister had already gone so I bailed too. My poor mother stuck with my dad for about another 10 months and then, she could take no more. My father went to Northern Ontario and so our home had disintegrated.

When I was a kid, I, like most other kids, felt our family would always be together. Now, within a matter of years, it was gone. We met at different times, at various locations, and pretended we were ok. As anyone who has experienced a break up of this sort, you will understand when I say life was never the same. This was the fuel that allowed the addiction to flare up out of control. No need to pretend anymore. All systems are "go".

From that time, until I got clean 16 years later, I made sure I never got close to a human being again. My father died before I was able to get clean so we'll have to do our talking in the afterlife. I have been married twice. My first marriage involved no children because I was childish enough to fill that role. It lasted seven years with me using most of the time, although I made some feeble attempts at getting clean. Not because I really wanted to but, at times, to get the heat off, I would abstain. My wife Rosemary was a good gal and her parents were equally as good. They treated me like their son and did everything they could to make me feel accepted. I look forward to seeing them in heaven too. I was clean 10 years when I remarried. My new wife had four daughters. I knew I had a big job on my hands but I was determined to give them the family life I wasn't able to appreciate. I loved my wife Judy and her four girls; Tracey, Trieste, Joey ad Ruth. I still do and believe they feel that way too. In fact, I know they do. Joey lived with me for 11 years until I moved out here, to Vancouver, in 2004. Tracey lives here in Vancouver so I see her regularly. Trieste and Ruth I don't see as much, but I do receive phone calls. I won't go into why our marriage dissolved because that is no ones business but "Our Family" and it will always be "Our Family", for better, not for worse. I am extremely proud of them all. I have learned, over the years, that we all make our share of mistakes but that does not change the fact that we were and are family, right down to the cats: Scruffy, Peekie Pie, the rabbits and the hamsters.

I have had some regrets throughout the years that I've been clean but they are nothing compared to the regrets and guilt I had when I was using. Our life does not always go the way we plan. Sometimes, it gets even better. In all your endeavors, acknowledge Him, and He will direct your path.

Cleaning our side of the street from the past is absolutely necessary if we are to live any kind of contented life today. We may not know where many people whom we jerked around are today but, when they do cross our path, we must try to make things right with them. If the opportunity is there and we avoid it, we will pay for it down the road. We can't let things pile up. Situations from the past, as I said, rob us of contentment in the present, and bring on fear of the future. One reason why I don't worry about the future is that God has delivered me this far clean, (with some bumps and bruises), so why should I not believe He has my future in His plan. I used to be like most addicts, very impatient, ready to jump in and make things happen in my time, if not before. Over the years I have been shown that all I can do is put out the effort I need to make something happen and, if it doesn't, perhaps my timing is not right. Maybe it was meant to be a delayed action rather than right then and there. Also, God has different ideas and He can't make me see them if I'm focused on my own thoughts of what I think the solution is.

For 15 years I worked as a driving instructor for Rite Way Driving School. The world's greatest driving school. Their slogan was; "The Right Way is the only way." That is a fact, in learning to drive or in learning anything in life. I used to tell my students I really enjoyed the job because it got me closer to God. Patience and faith are the two things you acquire in that job. You need patience with your students and other drivers on the road and faith that God will get you through the day alive. Fifteen years, working with some of the greatest people in the world, thanks all you guys. I still pray for everyone at Rite Way, new management included, because that job gave me an opportunity to work on the character defects I had and helped me understand what pressure was and how to cope with it.

From time to time I met people who were in recovery and were taking the Driver's Ed Course. I enjoyed being able to learn from them and perhaps help a little in regards to recovery. God works in mysterious ways, His wonders to perform. Getting me to retirement and reasonably sane are definitely examples of the wonders He has performed. Besides all that, happy and clean! I could not have achieved this on my own. Believe me. I could not have stayed clean, let alone happy. If you are going through tough times, just check how you and God are communicating. Perhaps it might be time to do some listening. He works through people too.

Dez, Azja and Nikki (Son)

Rhut

Shawn

Tash

Vance

Dave

Eagle

Andrew

Carmen

Jim

House 1

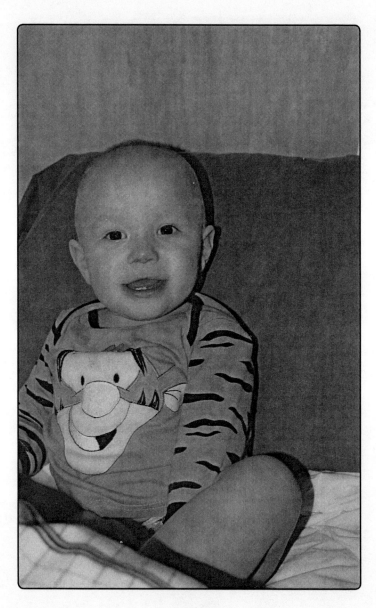

Keegan

House 2

Conrad

House 3

Cam

Tom

Chris

House 4

Tasha

Joy

Sarah

Mari and Lee

Gramhe

House 5

Justin

Gerry

Jordie

CHAPTER 5

We continued to take a look at ourselves on a daily basis and, when anything bothered us, we talked about it.

We continued to what? When the hell does this examination and changing stop? I want to be clean but I don't think I need to be perfect! This is getting to be a pain. When do I get a break from this? You say every day I have to look at me. I'm not using, what's the problem? This was me at different times in my recovery. Every time I started asking these questions, I eventually went back to using. I stopped asking these questions in 1971 and I haven't used since. To answer the first question, when does this examination and changing stop? NEVER! If it does stop, I stop staying clean. If staying clean is not the most important thing in my life, I can stop examining myself anytime I want to. The good news is I only have to examine me today. But I did the first four Recovery Values. Shouldn't that look after me for a few months? No? Why not? Because we have a habit of picking up some of our old games and doing re-runs. You played these games for years. Do you think they will go quietly into the garbage can and stay there? Our old attitudes and habits have created our personality over a period of time so they won't be easy to ditch. We have to remember that our old thinking ways created our old habits so, obviously, if we want to create new and better habits, we need new and healthier thinking ways. Come on now! What did you guys expect from me? Perfection? No, No, No, No, No, No. That's not something I, you, or any other addict needs to worry about. Why is that always our first reaction to change? No one ever even whispered the word perfection around me yet I always came back with "you want me to be perfect!" What I really meant was "I don't want to change anything! I'm ok the way I am." If I did change my attitude, I broke my arm patting myself on the back. I was 14 years old when I started to use and, emotionally, that was my reality when I got clean at 34 years old. I threw little tantrums just like a 14 year old when things upset me. This is a very tough reality to accept when we get clean. Certainly, at 34, there were many things I had learned and experienced that I didn't know when I was 14 but, for example, my ability to deal with disappointment was still that of a 14 years old. Just ask any of my bosses or relatives about that. They will agree. I was just a little kid if I didn't get what I thought should be mine. Most of us, including me, have to understand that changing is like rowing a boat upstream against the current. The second we stop rowing, we go backwards. Our old thinking ways and habits, when it comes to drugs, are just a swamp of mosquitoes. That is how drugs can breed in our head. When we experience disappointments or any type of pain, if our thinking isn't changing, we can convince ourselves that the answer is dope. Let's look at that for a minute, not just to get us off your back, but honestly. When did drugs ever improve your life? When? Perhaps it deadens the pain, but is that really making things better? The pain is still there, you just can't feel it. So the problem is still there and, by not dealing with it, it is getting worse. If you have muscle problems in your leg and you shoot some painkiller into it you can walk and even run on it. However, does that repair the muscle damage? It does? I'm glad you aren't my doctor. I would have been happy to have you as my doctor when I was using though. Unfortunately, there are some like that. The point is that pain, whether it is physical or mental, has to be dealt with. We seem to be ready to admit that we don't know how to fix our physical pain ourselves but, when it comes to emotional pain, which has our life out of control, we refuse to accept any help, other than drugs.

Let's start looking at the seven deadly sins again. This time, after I have been clean for a while. In my case, the longer I was clean, the more EGO told me I was ok now. You're clean so, what's the problem? Would I go to the dentist and have the decay drilled out of a tooth and then say; "that's it, I'm good to go. The decay is gone. No filling, just remove the decay?" Why then do I remove all the EGO from my using life and replace it with nothing? I'm very proud that I am and have been clean since 1971 but, am I proud that I have changed my thinking and my actions since then? Yes. I am, but, I could have done better and, I am doing better. We all can go through periods where we seem to be spinning our wheels but, as long as we don't pick up ay dope, we will eventually get tired of the scenery and decide to start moving forward again. If we have really been serious about Recovery Value 1 from the very beginning, not wanting to go back to dope will motivate us to get on with the job our High Power wants us to do. In the back of our mind, if we still think we can use, when we fall into a slump we will probably decide to use.

As I write this my guts are saying "man, am I ever grateful that I not only admitted I was powerless but I also accepted, from the very beginning, and I still do, that drugs meant death for me." It was more than just; "MY LIFE WAS A MESS", it was "ANY MORE DOPE AND MY LIFE IS AT AN END!" Perhaps you don't see things that way. Perhaps you think; "things were bad, but not that bad." Up till the 6th of June 1971, I felt the same way. I always thought; "when I decide to get clean again, I'll just get clean." I discovered it was not quite that easy. Even though I had been clean five separate times, for up to two years at one time, I couldn't get clean. I was stoned about two weeks on my last run and after that first two days I tried to stop. The guilt and remorse were so strong I had to use. For the first time in my addicted life I couldn't stop even when I decided I wanted to. This scared the hell out of me. I wasn't calling the shots anymore, drugs were. On the morning of June 6th, 1971, I came to with a shortage of breath and pain in my chest. I fell out of the filthy bed in my flop house room, hit the floor on my knees and, for the first time in my life, honestly and with no conditions, begged God to save my life. I have been clean ever since! I have also been ""Happy Clean"" 90 percent of the time. It is very simple; I apply the Recovery Values to my daily living and I stay clean and happy. Go through the motions and I just exist. When I apply the Recovery Values, my higher self gets even healthier. When I don't, it becomes EGO.

GREED

Over the years this has been a problem for me. Understanding the difference between wanting and needing has often been a struggle. When I first got clean I thought, "Now I can have any material thing I want!" Over the years, I discovered that all these little toys didn't satisfy me the way I thought they would. I am retired now and am enjoying my life here in beautiful Vancouver and, certainly, a few extra dollars help in that regard but only to the point where it gives me some free time to see what I can contribute in helping someone on the streets find a way out. I will go into this a little more in Recovery Value 6.

LUST

When I finally understood what a useless, frustrating game I was playing and, also, that some people were playing with me, I started to gain some control. I recognize a beautiful female when I see one today but I leave the games to someone else. This is definitely something that needs to be controlled one day at a time or it can eat us up. Remember, we aren't saints just yet. Maybe tomorrow eh? Not!

ANGER

Now that I've been clean awhile, how am I doing with anger? Believe me because I am being very honest when I say this, I very seldom get angry nowadays. I guess that at this stage of my life there isn't much that I can get angry about. I get a bit frustrated over some of the petty arguments that people have but I recognize that everyone is at a different stage of recovery and it's all part of learning how to live without dope. We can confront people about things we feel are holding them back from the good life but, just like me, until they are ready to look at themselves, the confrontation will probably result in nothing being solved. It also depends on whether the confrontation is done with love or; "I'm going to put you in your place." Whatever method you use, be prepared to get the same one back some day. We all go through days where we don't apply the Recovery Values to our life the way we should. When this happens, we will probably get on somebody's nerves. What goes around comes around, right?

GLUTTONY

I think another word for this is extremes. Over the years, one day at a time, I have begun to learn a little bit about moderation. There is not too much anymore that gets me running to the same crazy extremes that I used to. I guess, in time, between being clean awhile and old age, a person begins to mellow so that things are not always a crisis. I don't go on ice cream binges anymore or chocolate bar runs. Coffee can still be over used sometimes but, most days, three cups is about it. Life is good. I'm healthy enough that I can roller-blade from my apartment around the Sea Wall, which is about 30KM and, in a nice mild temperate climate like here in Vancouver, I also do a fair amount of walking. I am 75 years old but age is not something I think or worry about. Like Satchel Page, that great black baseball player said; "How old would you be if you didn't know how old you were?"

ENVY

I don't envy anyone or anything anymore. If I see someone who is a great example of how to live in this world, I simply try to do the same. I'm not sure how that person gets the results they get, but I get mine from following our Six Recovery Values. Pure and simple. I have read many self help books and I still do but for me, it all comes down to applying the Six Recovery Values to my life. I hope I don't sound too smug because I'm not trying to come off that way. If, after all these years of living drug free, I haven't found contentment, then I'm obviously doing something wrong. If I'm still fighting with the same demons today that I was fighting 20 years ago, perhaps I better change my approach to life. We all have to accept and change. This will remove envy.

LAZINESS (SLOTH)

Over the years, I certainly have been guilty of laziness. Since I've retired I have an acceptable excuse to be lazy. When I tell people I am retired, they just roll their eyes and say "must be nice." I then say "it is" and I sure mean it. It is really nice to have a flexible schedule. I hope everyone gets the opportunity to experience this. However, as a result of my schedule, I realized I now had the time to do some of the writing I've always wanted to do. I don't consider myself an award winning writer, since I didn't (thanks to drugs), finish high school. What you get here is simply one person's ideas and experiences on how to live as happy as possible, without the use of drugs. In Recovery Value 6, we look at how to let as many people as possible discover the same type of happiness.

Dwight-Rosemary

CHAPTER 6

With God and our friends, we tried to give other addicts what we have received and to follow these recovery values in our daily living.

If we have done something about applying the previous five recovery values to our life then we have something worth sharing with people who are still using, as well as people who have been clean for a while. Obviously, the more we know about the Recovery Values on a personal basis, the easier it will be to pass it on to others. Most of us get very excited about getting other people clean when we haven't really taken the time to understand what we have to do. There is more to it than throwing the drugs in the garbage. We can't be in grade one of elementary school and expect to suddenly have all the answers to life. Actually most of us thought we knew it all while we were still using so why wouldn't we have all the answers when we get clean? Not! Man, oh man, oh man. When I look back at where I was when I got clean! I was lost. If I'm still alive and "Happy Clean" twenty years from now I'm sure I will look back at where I am today and realize how lost I am right now. If I am growing in the Recovery Values, I should be able to see some progress. If we are clean from day one then the only value we can honestly say we completely have is Recovery Value 1. In order to open the door to the Recovery Values we have to accept what Recovery Value 1 says. Believe it and kick drugs out of our life, one day at a time. All types of drugs. If you are still using, you might be able to tell someone how to get clean but it's impossible to show them how. I guess it's your business if you are ready to settle for just telling people what to do, instead of showing them. Showing them, one day at a time, is the routine we need for them and for us. The only answers to problems I can honestly give someone are answers to problems of my own, which I discovered through trying to apply the Recovery Values to those problems. One thing I can't do is expect to have answers for everybody, for everything. I would like to think I can, but anyone who knows me can tell you, I can't. If you are anything like me, you'll look for answers that seem to be the easiest, not necessarily the best. One day at a time, honesty will make us search for the best. Something else we must make sure we don't do is guarantee anyone that their best high clean will be better than their best high stoned. We don't know what their best high was like. One thing we can guarantee is that their best high clean will be better than their best high stoned because it will be real, not plastic. Most addicts are not asking about the clean life because they are really enjoying the life they are now living. There quite likely are some court cases coming up, their families have thrown them out, they've been fired, or someone heavy is looking for them. Even though I told people I wanted help to get clean what I really wanted was some relief for awhile, from all my problems. When the problems were looked after, I wasn't as anxious to stay clean. I also thought that I should be able to live the rest of my life with no problems whatsoever. Reality was not one of my best assets when I got clean. In fact, reality was a word I tried very hard to avoid.

Over the years, I had conditioned myself to associate drugs with happy and reality with bummer. Most addicts have started to use very early in their life and as a result, find it impossible to think of high in the same sentence as clean. This is the big lie that drugs plant deeply in our brain. Drugs tell us that the only way to a problem-free party life is stoned. This is not social using folks, this is a constant buzz. In time, drugs, and our using friends, convince us that this continuous buzz is normal and that being clean is abnormal. Once we are convinced of this we will not listen to any other argument. Even when problems with family, law, education, and relationships with non users, overdoses and other medical related situations occur, drugs still have us convinced they are the answer to being happy. You may even be able to get an addict to agree that drugs are causing all these problems but they continue to use anyways. This is similar to showing the people who are building bigger bombs the destruction that the old bombs caused; they agree and continue working on new ones. We have stronger and more addictive and pleasure delivering drugs coming onto the market all the time so our battle sometimes looks like a losing one. It is only a losing battle if we all stop trying to fight the fight. I have discovered, even though it hurts and seems hopeless, that showing people that you care and are ready to help when they are ready to receive, is the only door open to us. Once drugs do for an addict what the addict can't do for him or herself, no amount of arguing will change their thinking. Some people have certain ideas about prevention. I will talk about my ideas later on in this chapter.

With God and our Friends, we tried to give other addicts what we have received. Just exactly what have I received since I've been clean? Number 1: I'm alive. Not just existing, but alive. Every year, when I go for my annual medical check-up, my doctor says "when I'm your age, I hope I'm as healthy as you are." I Inline skate for an hour everyday that the weather allows and, when it doesn't, I ice skate or bike. Perhaps people think I am as crazy as a loon but, mentally, I feel good also. I am grateful to be alive, clean, and healthy. What more could I ask for? I live in the greatest city in the world, Vancouver, and if you know of one that is better, let me know, and I'll move there. There are people on the street that I can talk to every day who need help. Not all of them want help of course but, if they want to listen, I can tell them about me. If they don't I can still enjoy the scenery.

It is so nice to wake up every day free from fear, pain, hate, hunger, envy, or any other of the many negatives that used to be part of my morning. If, from day to day, any of the above comes into my life, I simply have to talk to someone; talk to my God and then change or accept the situation. Seldom do I have to accept a situation. Usually, I can change it. Each of us is, in most cases, responsible for the situation we are in. If we are really serious about being clean we will do what we have to do so we can stay clean that day. There are days when I wish I could blame others for my situation, but I can't. At this point in my life, I'm too selfish to let other people put me on a bummer. That doesn't mean I can use and abuse people. It simply means I am responsible for my own happiness, as are you. If I'm not content, I have to look at why. Is it something I'm doing wrong that goes against what the Recovery Values tell me or, is it people who would rather be miserable and blame me for it? Honest now. I have to be honest. If my conscience is clean, I'll be free of fear. That is the simple answer for me. I may think I am right about some situation but, if my guts don't feel good, then I need to talk to God and another human being to get their feedback. I have to listen to my guts, God, and people. Then I have to follow the advice.

Attempted to give addicts what we have received. What if they don't want what we have received? Until an addict really feels pain and fear, they probably will not be too anxious to look at or accept anything we have to offer. They will gladly accept money, a get out of jail free card, or anything else that will immediately improve their situation. When you tell them this is not the type of help you have in mind you will then discover how serious they are about getting clean. If you are fortunate enough to talk to someone who simply wants to stop using and change their lifestyle, it will be very easy to help them. They will be very eager to try on the Recovery Values. However, these people are in the minority when it comes to wanting help. The others will have to dig deeper into the dead end garbage dump before they are ready, if they don't die or get killed first. This is the reality of a user.

I was offered help in July 1967. After four years of playing games with the help, it took the fear of dying to finally drive home the message; that I am not fire proof! Most of us will not be ready to do business until we are completely cornered like a rat. As long as drugs appear to meet our needs, getting clean will not be our number one priority. Until we have squeezed every drop of pleasure we can from drugs, we will be its prisoners. Drugs will run our life and laugh at us. Addicts, like me, screamed; "It's my life! Leave me alone to enjoy it!" Oh, yeah? Oh, yeah? I didn't want anyone to tell me what to do yet drugs told me every day what to do. I thought I was free. I was about as free as someone doing life without parole. Do drugs, do drugs, do drugs, do drugs, do drugs, do drugs, do drugs, do drugs!!! About 80 percent of people who are in jail are there because of drugs, and they are still doing drugs. They will get out one day, if someone doesn't kill them first, and continue doing drugs and go back inside again. This is just one example of drugs running a person's life and they still don't see it; total control of our thinking and living. You may say "I haven't gone that far!" and I will reply "YET!" How many days have you gone without using or thinking about using lately? Most users who still have a job and some material toys will say "I can take it or leave it!" Yeah? If that's the case then why do you chose to take it? "I can afford it. My life is not being affected. I am continually moving ahead in my job. My health is good. My family and friends love me. I have no emotional problems. I sleep and I love myself and my life." Oh yeah? Oh yeah? Have you talked to any of the people who are or have been involved in your life lately? Do they see things the same way you do? Perhaps you are looking at the way things used to me. Honestly. Are you happy with the road you are on? Or could things be a bit better? Don't you think researching life without drugs might be worth a try? What have you experienced so far in life? Is it good enough for you? If your life ended today, what would people have in their memory about you, or me? At one point in my life, that was enough to get me stoned. I knew I was doing nothing with my life. I knew for sure that I wasn't a genius but I also knew I could do a lot more with my life than I was doing. Stoned, I would tell you all the great things I would do. Clean, I hid in my shell. Drugs were my guts; without them I was a wimp. A lot of good people will never know what they might have accomplished, because they won't throw away their crutch. You haven't been conned until you have been conned by drugs. The greatest lie in the world! Drugs have done such an expert job of convincing us we can't live without them. No amount of solid facts showing us exactly the opposite will make any sense to us while we're stoned. Drugs are the master! We are the slaves! When we lose our value as an advertising tool for drugs, we are then discarded like an old shoe. You're worn out and you stink; goodbye! Perhaps this sounds a little dramatic, but is it?

Drugs do not want to be associated with losers so, if you are a constant problem to society, your using friends will say you are the problem, not drugs. They will spread the word very quickly and you will find yourself by yourself. You say "my friends would never do that!" Just watch my man. Just watch. The people you call friends are just people you get stoned with. When was the last time you really had a friend? If all my friends are users, and we all are using so we can be someone we're not, how do we know who the other people are? Is our character becoming the same, stoned or clean? Who is the real us? I had no idea who I was. I became so many different people during my using career. It would depend on what crowd I was with, as to who I was that day. Strawberry fields, where nothing is real. Who wanted real? Real hurt too much. Who used the expression "get real" the way we did? Lost! Lost! Lost! My friends and I were all Hollywood stars. Or was it T.V. stars? Or was it marriage counselors? No it was defensive drivers, wasn't it? What about "father knows best", experts on religion, the law, national defense, nutrition (with a joint in our mouth), as well as the world's greatest fortune tellers? These were just some of our specialties. When we had informed everyone in this group of friends about the secrets to life, we moved onto another group. Or were we moved on? Not quite sure about that. Many times I found myself in a different city, in a bar, picking the label on the bottle, trying to figure out why all my good advice didn't seem to work on me.

Another method that doesn't work on addicts is telling them that drugs will kill them. How could anything that makes you feel so good possibly kill you? This is where the little kid's reasoning emerges. People who have been using for years, over dosed many times, been beaten up, stabbed, shot, locked up in rubber rooms, still insist drugs won't kill them. When someone they know dies, they will say it wasn't the dope. It was that the person who died didn't know the proper way of using it. Or they may say it was the person who sold the dope, sold bad dope, and then go and buy some from the same person. Impossible you say? Not! Insane, yes!

Prevention. Is there such a thing? Short of destroying every possible substance that can get you stoned, I don't think there is. That sounds rather discouraging doesn't it? Reality is, there will always be drugs in this world. Does that mean everyone has to use them? No! However, as long as there are people who don't think they have the personality or talents of superstars and seem to be tongue tied in public, there will always be a market for drugs. My opinion is that drugs are a personality escape hatch. When I am stoned, drugs allowed me to be the person I would like to be in real life;

the cool, relaxed, smooth talker, knowledgeable, everyday superstar. If I arrived at a party late and clean I would get as much drugs into me in a short time so I could catch up to everyone else and not have that old feeling of not being "with it". Then I could start being the star of the show. The real me was the paranoid guy in the corner. The star was the stoned me. The paranoid me thought the whole world was looking at me. The stoned me did everything I could to get the whole world looking at me. Personality change! Big time! What I am trying to say is that if you know someone or you are someone who fits this description, there is a very good chance drugs are or will become a problem. There are some people who can go to a party, completely clean, and appear to have a terrific time. They don't feel out of place and even contribute to the party. That was not me. If I couldn't get stoned, I wouldn't go.

So, what can parents do to try to prevent the above from happening? I will give you my opinion. It may not be right, but it is my opinion. Looking back at my childhood, I believe that, up to the age of nine, I felt pretty together and confident that I could compete with my friends and surroundings. Over the next three years we moved a few times and I never felt that comfort level again. Things were changing too quickly for me to keep up. There seemed to be less time with the whole family. Everyone seemed to be doing their own thing. My brother and sister were now in high school. They had new friends and didn't include me in the things they did. That is understandable now but, at that time, I started feeling left out and different. My brother and sister kept saying "oh Norm, you wouldn't understand" or "you can't go, because you're too young." My parents also seemed to be busy all the time. Perhaps this was not the way the picture was, but that was the way it appeared to me.

Then, I ended up in high school, with an even larger level of competition. Kids that were better athletes, better students, and better at socializing. A school dance was as much fun as a trip to the dentist. Man I felt awkward. My sister tried to give me dancing lessons at home. That never works too well, folks. I should say that for me it didn't work too well. Then, an amazing thing happened. At a school dance someone turned me onto drugs and the rest, as they say, was history. I couldn't dance enough. I asked girls to dance that I usually could not even say hello to. I couldn't understand why we had to stop dancing at 1 PM. I had finally discovered life. From then on I was never alone. Do you follow? I managed to scrape by in school for the next four years because my friends, and my friend, were there. Reality and my family were out. Addictions, and Norm, were together and growing. No one understood me but my friends and my friend. I began to feel that anyone who didn't like my friends, or my friend, didn't like me. This of course included my parents, who were having their own problems. By this time, no amount of talking, lecturing, yelling, pleading or bargaining could remove drugs from my life. I was 16 now and grown up.

Today kids are being turned on at seven and eight years old. This doesn't give parents much time to try and drug proof them. Parents, nowadays, are on a life escalator that doesn't stop. Everyone is working. Everyone is busy. Everyone is tired. I am not being critical now. I am just describing what life is like for most parents. I feel for parents today. Most of them feel swamped. I am not trying to tell people how to raise their children. I will only say; please try to sit down with your kids and tell them and show them you love them. Do everything you can to make them feel your love. Having the responsibility of guiding someone's little life in the right direction in this world is the most important of all human responsibilities, I think. Perhaps, before people consider creating a child, they should ask themselves if they are really prepared for the time and the amount of love that will be required, to give this little person the tools they need to deal with life. Whether we want to accept it or not, these little guys are depending on us, to show them the way. When they start to cause us problems it's a little late to say "we wish we never had these kids."

The most important aspect in the family is that we can show love if we are loving. We can't play the game of pretending we are a family. It has to be real. If we are ever going to stop this mad roller coaster that chews up people's lives and spits them out, we have to start at the beginning of each life. Try to…no…give your kids the love that you perhaps missed out on. Believe me, if you never give them anything else, it will be all they will ever need to meet life head on. Nothing else will do the job. Love is the greatest. Encouragement is one of the ingredients of love. Kids have to be told and shown that losing or failing is not the end of the world. After a time out to look at why they missed the mark, they can get back up and get after it again. One common flaw with addicts is giving up on something that is worthwhile. If only they could take the same attitude towards dope. They quit on the wrong things. If kids begin to feel they can't compete, and start feeling negative and sorry for themselves, they are easy pickings for drugs. Self confident people don't need additives.

As I said earlier, I know parents are worn out. Raising a family is not a robot's job.. However, they are your kids and you owe them. Not clothes, food, shelter, dancing lessons, skates or a football. You owe them the love they need to cope in this world. All those other things are just part of the package in this realm of reality. Aside from the clothes, food and shelter, they could live without the other stuff, if they were truly loved. You may scoff at that, but don't scoff till you try it. When kids really feel loved, they can accept life's disappointments and understand the reason why. They just want to feel proud of their parents, love them, and be loved. I wanted to be proud of my dad but as an alcoholic preacher, he heaped a pile of disgrace on our family. Today I can forgive him, because my life was not a brilliant design for living either.

Parents may not like this fact, but impressionable kids are going to follow the path their parents are on. As kids, we all think our parents can do nothing wrong. Honesty and love, I feel, are the two most important gifts you can share with them. Kids may seem to be very demanding at times but all they are saying is "please help me, I'm scared." Try to recognize that. They aren't adults, they're kids. So folks, don't get confused. The directions are pretty simple; love and honesty. How you do that is your business, but do it. They're counting on it, need it and deserve it. I believe in parents. You can do it. If your kids do get lost for awhile, at least you won't have to wonder about what more could have been done. If the love is real and the honesty is real, you shouldn't have any guilt to haunt you. Also, if love and honesty are real, the kids will know in their guts that you gave everything you could. One day, it will make sense to them. They will throw their dope away, get real, and start giving you back some of the love you gave them. What goes around comes around. Until then, perhaps the God of your understanding can carry you through. It all starts at home folks, for better or for worse.

As the intellectuals say, (having said that), you don't want to turn your kids into little wimps either! If you do, drug users in their school will intimidate them to the point that they will use drugs in self defense. Kids in this society have to be able to stand solid against drug intimidation. They will discover, very early, who the users are and who the non users are in their school and in their neighborhood. The users look and act tough but its drugs that give them this image. If your kids are impressed with this and want to be part of it, they are done. To be part, you have to use. If these users were so tough, they wouldn't need dope to prove it. It is because they are exactly the opposite that they use drugs. Until your kids feel confident enough to hold their own with users, they might be wise to stay close to their clean friends and together in numbers. Don't walk the streets alone. Users have that false courage from drugs and, to impress their friends, they could try to raise their image by beating-up someone who is by themselves. Numbers work both ways. Follow?

Real communication between you and your kids will be the difference between them and avoiding drugs or getting sucked into it. You have to develop an open and honest dialogue with them. They have to be able to feel they can tell you anything in confidence and that you won't blab it all over the school. If someone needs to be busted, an anonymous tip to the police will do the job. Don't put your kids in danger by trying to be a neighborhood hero. If you live in a city, there are many agencies that can help you discover what the drug of choice is in your particular area, (if your kids don't already know), and also what areas to avoid in the city. Drugs are everywhere but more congested in some areas than others. Tell your kids that unless there is a good reason for them to be there, they need to stay out. They don't fit in so they'll stand out like a sore thumb. Remember; real communication from them to you and you to them! When the secrets start, the problems start! You don't have to know everything about their social life but you do have to know who their friends are. There are also open meetings of Narcotics Anonymous that you and your kids can attend to hear firsthand from recovering addicts; what caused them to use, what happened, and how things are now that they don't use. Our House has online meetings which can be accessed through our website at www.Sanity365.com. We can also be reached on Facebook through Our House Vancouver. We presently have one afternoon meeting a week as well as five morning meetings per week. Our long term goal is to have a crisis line to talk to anyone with a problem including parents, siblings, partners, or anyone in the helping profession. We realize that, at the present time, what we may do will hardly put a dent in the drug problem but united, with dedicated others, we believe what we can do is put hope in the hearts of users as well as the families who stand helplessly by, praying for answers.

CPSIA information can be obtained at www.ICGtesting.com
Printed in the USA
LVOW131043151212

311731LV00001B/3/P